Mark Di Suvero

Mark Di Suvero

OPEN SECRET:

SCULPTURE 1990-92

Poems selected by the artist

GAGOSIAN GALLERY

In association with Richard Bellamy

RIZZOLI
NEW YORK

Space has been the most important element in

sculpture for me. We see space stereoscopically (with two eyes)

yet almost all photographs see monocularly (with one eye).

To replace this lost dimension, I have thought to add poems I love

and that have changed my life, so that the bridge between the poem

and the photo-image becomes the true reality, a voyage of

the imagination in your mind's eye. You may see the materiality,

spatiality, and participant's movement disappear in a photo:

between the photo and the poem is the music—meaning of this

sculptor's life.

MdiS

ALL THINGS CONFINE

All things
Crowd me in!
I am so wide!

After the unshapen
Have I grasped
In everlasting time.

I have caught it.
It has cast me
Wider than wide!

Me is too narrow
All else!
You know this well
You that have been there too.

HADEWIJCH

L'Allumé, 1989-1992. Painted steel. 35'4" x 35'4" x 15'9" (10.8 x 10.8 x 4.8 m)

ALLE DINGE

Alle dinge
Zijn mi te inge,
Ik ben zo wijd:
Om een ongeschepen
Heb ik begrepen
In eeuwigen tijd.

Ik heb 't gevaan.
Het heeft mi ontdaan
Widere dan wijd;
Mi es te inge al el;
Dat wette wel
Gi dies ook daar zijt.

HADEWIJCH

L'Allumé

DAWN

Dawn in New York has
four columns of mire
and a hurricane of black pigeons
splashing in the putrid waters.

Dawn in New York groans
on enormous fire escapes
searching between the angles
for spikenards of drafted anguish.

Dawn arrives and no one receives it in his mouth
because morning and hope are impossible there:
sometimes the furious swarming coins
penetrate like drills and devour abandoned children.

Those who go out early know in their bones
there will be no paradise or loves that bloom and die:
they know they will be mired in numbers and laws,
in mindless games, in fruitless labors.

The light is buried under chains and noises
in an impudent challenge to rootless science.
And crowds stagger sleeplessly through the boroughs
as if they had just escaped a shipwreck of blood.

FEDERICO GARCÍA LORCA

Johnny Appleseed, 1987-1992. Steel. 23'6" x 22' x 44' (7.2 x 6.7 x 11.2 m)

LA AURORA

La Aurora de Nueva York tiene
cuatro columnas de cieno
y un huracán de negras palomas
que chapotean las aguas podridas.

La aurora de Nueva York gime
por las inmensas escaleras
buscando entre las aristas
nardos de angustia dibujada.

La aurora llega y nadie la recibe en su boca
porque allí no hay mañana ni esperanza posible.
A veces las monedas en enjambres furiosos
taladran y devoran abandonados niños.

Los primeros que salen comprenden con sus huesos
que no habrá paraíso ni amores deshojados;
saben que van al cieno de números y leyes,
a los juegos sin arte, a sudores sin fruto.

La luz es sepultada por cadenas y ruidos
en impúdico reto de ciencia sin raíces.
Por los barrios hay gentes que vacilan insomnes
como recién salidas de un naufragio de sangre.

FEDERICO GARCÍA LORCA

Johnny Appleseed

from THE WAY OF LIFE

The surest test if a man be sane
Is if he accepts life whole, as it is,
Without needing by measure or touch to understand
The measureless untouchable source
Of its images,
The measureless untouchable source
Of its substances,
The source which, while it appears dark emptiness,
Brims with a quick force
Farthest away
And yet nearest at hand
From oldest time unto this day,
Charging its images with origin:
What more need I know of the origin
Than this?

LAO TZU

Preceding pages and above: *Lao Tzu*, 1991. Steel. 29'6" x 16'5" x 36'5" (9 x 5 x 11 m)

A NOISELESS PATIENT SPIDER

A noiseless patient spider,
I mark'd where on a little promontory it stood isolated,
Mark'd how to explore the vacant vast surrounding,
It launch'd forth filament, filament, filament, out of itself,
Ever unreeling down, ever tirelessly speeding them.

And you O my soul where you stand,
Surrounded, detached, in measureless oceans of space,
Ceaselessly musing, venturing, throwing, seeking the spheres to connect them,
Till the bridge you will need be form'd, till the ductile anchor hold,
Till the gossamer thread you fling catch somewhere, O my soul.

WALT WHITMAN

Opposite: *Extase,* 1991. Steel. 74'3" x 34'4" x 35'4" (23 x 10.5 x 10.8 m)

Extase

UNMARKED BOXES

Don't grieve. Anything you lose comes round
in another form. The child weaned from mother's milk
now drinks wine and honey mixed.

God's joy moves from unmarked box to unmarked box,
from cell to cell. As rainwater, down into flowerbed.
As roses, up from ground.
Now it looks like a plate of rice and fish,
now a cliff covered with vines,
now a horse being saddled.
It hides within these,
till one day it cracks them open.

Part of the self leaves the body when we sleep
and changes shape. You might say, "Last night
I was a cypress tree, a small bed of tulips,
a field of grapevines." Then the phantasm goes away.
You're back in the room.
I don't want to make any one fearful.
Hear what's behind what I say.

Tatatumtum tatum tatadum.
There's the light gold of wheat in the sun
and the gold of bread made from that wheat.
I have neither. I'm only talking about them,

as a town in the desert looks up
at stars on a clear night.

RUMI

Rumi, 1991. Steel. 24' x 8'9" (7.3 x 2.7 m)

Opposite and above: *Rumi*

SONNET 165

Stay, shadow of contentment too short-lived,
illusion of enchantment I most prize,
fair image for whom happily I die,
sweet fiction for whom painfully I live.

If to your charms attracted I submit,
obedient, like steel to magnet fly,
by what logic do you flatter and entice,
only to flee, a taunting fugitive?

Tis no triumph that you so smugly boast
that I fell victim to your tyranny;
though from encircling bonds that held you fast

your elusive form too readily slipped free,
and though to my arms you are forever lost,
you are prisoner in my fantasy.

Deténte, sombra de mi bien esquivo,
imagen del hechizo que más quiero,
bella ilusión por quien alegre muero,
dulce ficción por quien penosa vivo.

    Si al imán de tus gracias, atractivo,
sirve mi pecho de obediente acero,
¿para qué me enamoras lisonjero
si has de burlarme luego fugitivo?

    Mas blasonar no puedes, satisfecho,
de que triunfa de mí tu tiranía:
que aunque dejas burlado el lazo estrecho

    que tu forma fantástica ceñía,
poco importa burlar brazos y pecho
si te labra prisión mi fantasía.

SOR JUANA INÉS DE LA CRUZ

Esope, 1990. Steel. 11'5 ^{1}/$_4$" x 32'4 ^{1}/$_2$" x 13'7 ^{1}/$_2$" (3.5 x 9.9 x 4.2 m)

Yoga, 1991. Steel & stainless steel. 29'6¹/₂" x 31'2" (9 x 9.5 m)

TRUTH: Balade De Bon Conseyl

Flee fro the prees, and dwelle with sothfastnesse,
Suffyce unto thy good, though hit be smal;
For hord hath hate, and climbing tikelnesse,
Prees hath envye, and wele blent overal;
Savour no more than thee bihove shal;
Werk wel thy-self, that other folk canst rede;
And trouthe thee shal delivere, hit is not drede.

Tempest thee noght al croked to redresse,
In trust of hir that turneth as a bal:
Gret reste stant in litel besinesse;
And eek be war to sporne ageyn en al;
Stryve noght, as doth the crokke with the wal.
Daunte thy-self, that dauntest otheres dede;
And trouthe thee shal delivere, hit is not drede.

That thee is sent, receyve in buxumnesse,
The wrastling for this worlde axeth a fal.
Hir nis non hoom, her nis but wildernesse:
Forth, pilgrim, forth! Forth, beste, out of thy stal!
Know thy contree, look up, thank God of al;
Hold the hye wey, and lat thy gost thee lede;
And trouble thee shal delivere, hit is no drede.

Envoy

Therfore, thou vache, leve thyn old wrecchednesse
Unto the worlde; leve now to be thral;
Crye him mercy, that of his hy goodnesse
Made thee of noght, and in especial
Draw unto him, and pray in general
For thee, and eek for other, hevenlich mede;
And trouthe thee shal delivere, hit is no drede.

CHAUCER

TRUTH: A Ballad of Good Counsel

Flee from the crowd and dwell in truthfulness
Let your things suffice, though they be small,
For hoarding is hatred and climbing fickleness
Crowds breed envy, deceiving overall.
Savor no more than will to you befall,
Rule yourself well, so that others may hear,
And truth shall deliver you, there is no fear.

Do not vex yourself all crime to redress
Trusting Fortune, which rolls like a ball;
Great rest stands in little busyness.
Be wary, therefore, of kicking at an awl.
Strive not as does the pitcher with the wall.
Rule yourself, if you have another's ear
And truth shall deliver you, there is no fear.

What is sent to you, receive with thankfulness;
Your wrestling for this world asks for a fall;
Here is no home, here is but wilderness:
Forth, pilgrim, forth! Forth, beast, out of your stall!
Know your true home, look up, thank God for all.
Hold the high way, let your spirit pioneer
And truth shall deliver you, there is no fear.

Therefore, my friend, leave your old wretchedness.
Forget the world, leave off being thrall.
Cry to Him mercy, Who of His high goodness
Made you of nought, made you special.
Draw near to him and pray in general
For your own reward and for others dear;
And truth shall deliver you, there is no fear.

CHAUCER

Yoga

SONNET 94

They that have power to hurt and will do none,
That do not do the thing they most do show,
Who, moving others, are themselves as stone,
Unmovèd, cold, and to temptation slow—
They rightly do inherit Heaven's graces
And husband nature's riches from expense.
They are the lords and owners of their faces,
Others but stewards of their excellence.
The summer's flower is to the summer sweet,
Though to itself it only live and die,
But if that flower with base infection meet,
The basest weed outbraves his dignity.
    For sweetest things turn sourest by their deeds.
    Lilies that fester smell far worse than weeds.

SHAKESPEARE

Above and following pages: *Caramba!* 1984-1990. Steel. 11'9" x 8'6" x 18'6" (3.7 x 2.6 x 5.6 m)

AS KINGFISHERS CATCH FIRE...

As kingfishers catch fire, dragonflies dráw fláme;

As tumbled over rim in roundy wells

Stones ring; like each tucked string tells, each hung bell's

Bow swung finds tongue to fling out broad its name;

Each mortal thing does one thing and the same:

Deals out that being indoors each one dwells;

Selves——goes itself; *myself* it speaks and spells,

Crying *Whát I dó is me: for that I came.*

GERARD MANLEY HOPKINS

Tendresse, 1989-1990. (Detail) Steel. 29'6" x 21'4" x 30'9" (9 x 6.5 x 9.4 m)

Tendresse

Tendresse

THEY FLE FROM ME THAT SOMETYME DID ME SEKE

They fle from me that sometyme did me seke

With naked fote stalking in my chambre.

I have sene theim gentill tame and meke

That nowe are wyld and do not remembre

That sometyme they put theimself in daunger

To take bred at my hand; and nowe they raunge

Besely seking with a continuell chaunge.

Thancked be fortune, it hath ben othrewise

Twenty tymes better; but ons in speciall,

In thyn arraye after a pleasaunt gyse,

When her lose gowne from her shoulders did fall,

And she me caught in her armes long and small;

Therewithall swetely did me kysse,

And softely saide, dere hert, howe like you this?

It was no dreme: I lay brode waking.

But all is torned thorough my gentilnes

Into a straunge fasshion of forsaking;

And I have leve to goo of her goodenes,

And she also to use new fangilnes.

But syns that I so kyndely ame served,

I would fain knowe what she hath deserved.

SIR THOMAS WYATT

Tools with Dreams, 1990–1992. (Detail) Steel with wood base. 9'4" x 6'6" x 5'3" (2.9 x 2 x 1.6 m)

Tools with Dreams

Tools with Dreams

DRINKING ALONE UNDER THE MOON

A pot of wine among flowers.

I drink alone, nobody near.

I raise my jar to the moon: come share!

With my shadow, we would be three.

Ah, but the moon cares not for drink,

And my shadow's just following me around.

For a moment only moon, shadow, myself

    together.

Pleasure must be sought in spring.

I sing, and the moon is moving on.

I dance, my shadow trips and stumbles!

When sober, we all work together.

When drunk, everyone goes their own way.

Then let us make vows to wander

    away from the world and its ties

And meet again later at the end of the Milky Way.

LI PO

Rainbow Measurer, 1992. Steel & stainless steel. 53 ¹/₂ x 87 x 56" (1.4 x 2.2 x 1.4 m)

Following pages: *Petaluma Studio*

from CANTO I

Nel mezzo del cammin di nostra vita
mi ritrovai per una selva oscura,
ché la diritta via era smarrita.

Ahi quanto a dir qual era è cosa dura
esta selva selvaggia e aspra e forte
che nel pensier rinova la paura!

Tant' è amara che poco è più morte;
ma per trattar del ben ch'i' vi trovai,
dirò de l'altre cose ch'i' v'ho scorte.

Io non so ben ridir com' i' v'intrai,
tant' era pien di sonno a quel punto
che la verace via abbandonai.

from CANTO I

Halfway in the journey that is our life
I came to myself in the darkest of woods.
I had lost the straight path that leads away from night.

How difficult it is to tell of, crude
And savage, harsh, mired in bramble and thicket.
Even to recall it brings back fear.

Death itself is not nearly so severe.
But to register the good and great I found there
Let me tell further what I witnessed.

I cannot clearly say how I entered this wood:
I was weighted by sleep at the time and place
Where I abandoned the right true path.

DANTE

Vivaldi, 1992. Steel. 38' x 40' (11.6 x 12.2 m)

Left and above: *Spring Rain*, 1992. Steel. 38'10" x 37' x 37' (11.9 x 11.3 x 11.3 m)

ABEND

Der Abend wechselt langsam die Gewänder,
die ihm ein Rand von alten Bäumen hält;
du schast: und von dir scheiden sich die Länder,
ein himmelfahrendes und eins, das fällt;

und lassen dich, zu keinem ganz gehörend,
nicht ganz so dunkel wie das Haus, das schweigt,
nicht ganz so sicher Ewiges beshwörend
wie das, was Stern wird jede Nacht und steigt;

und lassen dir (unsäglich zu entwirrn)
dein Leben, bang und riesenhaft und reifend,
so daß es, bald begrenzt und bald begreifend,
abwechselnd Stein in dir wird und Gestirn.

EVENING

Slowly now the evening changes his garments
held for him by a rim of ancient trees;
you gaze: and the landscape divides and leaves you,
one sinking and one rising toward the sky.

And you are left, to none belonging wholly,
not so dark as a silent house, nor quite
so surely pledged unto eternity
as that which grows to star and climbs the night.

To you is left (unspeakably confused)
your life, gigantic, ripening, full of fears,
so that it, now hemmed in, now grasping all,
is changed in you by turns to stone and stars.

RAINER MARIA RILKE

Schubert Sonata, 1992. Steel. 22' x 19' (6.7 x 5.8 m)

Opposite and above: *Schubert Sonata*

THE FORCE THAT THROUGH THE GREEN FUSE
DRIVES THE FLOWER

The force that through the green fuse drives the flower

Drives my green age; that blasts the roots of trees

Is my destroyer.

And I am dumb to tell the crooked rose

My youth is bent by the same wintry fever.

The force that drives the water through the rocks

Drives my red blood; that dries the mouthing streams

Turns mine to wax.

And I am dumb to mouth unto my veins

How at the mountain spring the same mouth sucks.

The hand that whirls the water in the pool

Stirs the quicksand; that ropes the blowing wind

Hauls my shroud sail.

And I am dumb to tell the hanging man

How of my clay is made the hangman's lime.

The lips of time leech to the fountain head;

Love drips and gathers, but the fallen blood

Shall calm her sores.

And I am dumb to tell a weather's wind

How time has ticked a heaven round the stars.

And I am dumb to tell the lover's tomb

How at my sheet goes the same crooked worm.

DYLAN THOMAS

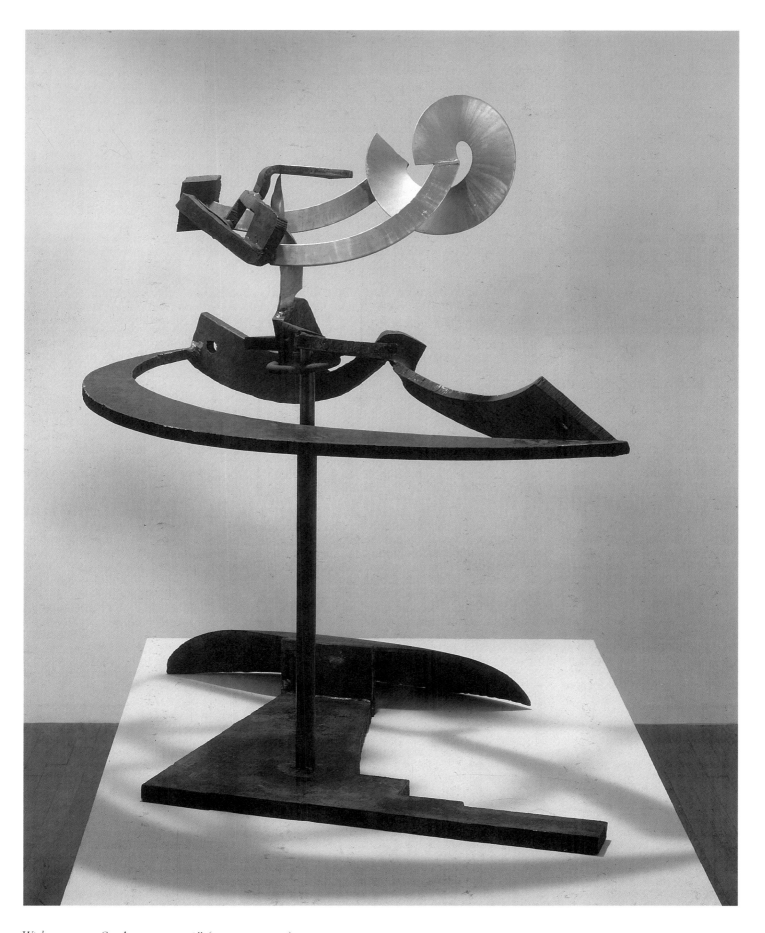

Wishtree, 1990. Steel. 60 x 45 x 48" (1.5 x 1.1 x 1.2 m)

TO A FRIEND WHOSE WORK HAS COME TO NOTHING

Now all the truth is out,
Be secret and take defeat
From any brazen throat,
For how can you compete,
Being honour bred, with one
Who, were it proved he lies,
Were neither shamed in his own
Nor in his neighbours' eyes?
Bred to a harder thing
Than Triumph, turn away
And like a laughing string
Whereon mad fingers play
Amid a place of stone,
Be secret and exult,
Because of all things known
That is most difficult.

W. B. YEATS

Nux, 1988-1992. Steel. 53 1/2 x 79 x 36" (136 x 201 x 91 cm)

OF ALL THE SOUNDS
DESPATCHED ABROAD

Of all the Sounds despatched abroad,
There's not a Charge to me
Like that old measure in the Boughs—
That phraseless Melody—
The Wind does—working like a Hand,
Whose fingers Comb the Sky—
Then quiver down—with tufts of Tune—
Permitted Gods, and me—

Inheritance, it is, to us—
Beyond the Art to Earn—
Beyond the trait to take away
By Robber, since the Gain
Is gotten not of fingers—
And inner than the Bone—
Hid golden, for the whole of Days,
And even in the Urn,
I cannot vouch the merry Dust
Do not arise and play
In some odd fashion of its own,
Some quainter Holiday,

When Winds go round and round in Bands—
And thrum upon the door,
And Birds take places, overhead,
To bear them Orchestra.

I crave Him grace of Summer Boughs,
If such an Outcast be—
Who never heard that fleshless Chant—
Rise—solemn—on the Tree,
As if some Caravan of Sound
Off Deserts, in the Sky,
Had parted Rank,
Then knit, and swept—
In Seamless Company—

EMILY DICKINSON

Ojibway, 1991. Steel & stainless steel. 20 x 21¹/₂ x 16¹/₄" (51 x 55 x 41 cm)

LA CALLE

Es una calle larga y silenciosa.
Ando en tinieblas y tropiezo y caigo
y me levanto y piso con pies ciegos
las piedras mudas y las hojas secas
y alguien detrás de mí también las pisa:
si me detengo, se detiene;
si corro, corre. Vuelvo el rostro: nadie.
Todo está oscuro y sin salida,
y doy vueltas y vueltas en esquinas
que dan siempre a la calle
donde nadie me espera ni me sigue,
donde yo sigo a un hombre que tropieza
y se levanta y dice al verme: nadie.

THE STREET

A long and silent street.
I walk in blackness and I stumble and fall
and rise, and I walk blind, my feet
stepping on silent stones and dry leaves.
Someone behind me also stepping on stones, leaves:
if I slow down, he slows;
if I run, he runs. I turn: nobody.
Everything dark and doorless.
Turning and turning among these corners
which lead forever to the street
where nobody waits for, nobody follows me,
where I pursue a man who stumbles
and rises and says when he sees me: nobody.

OCTAVIO PAZ

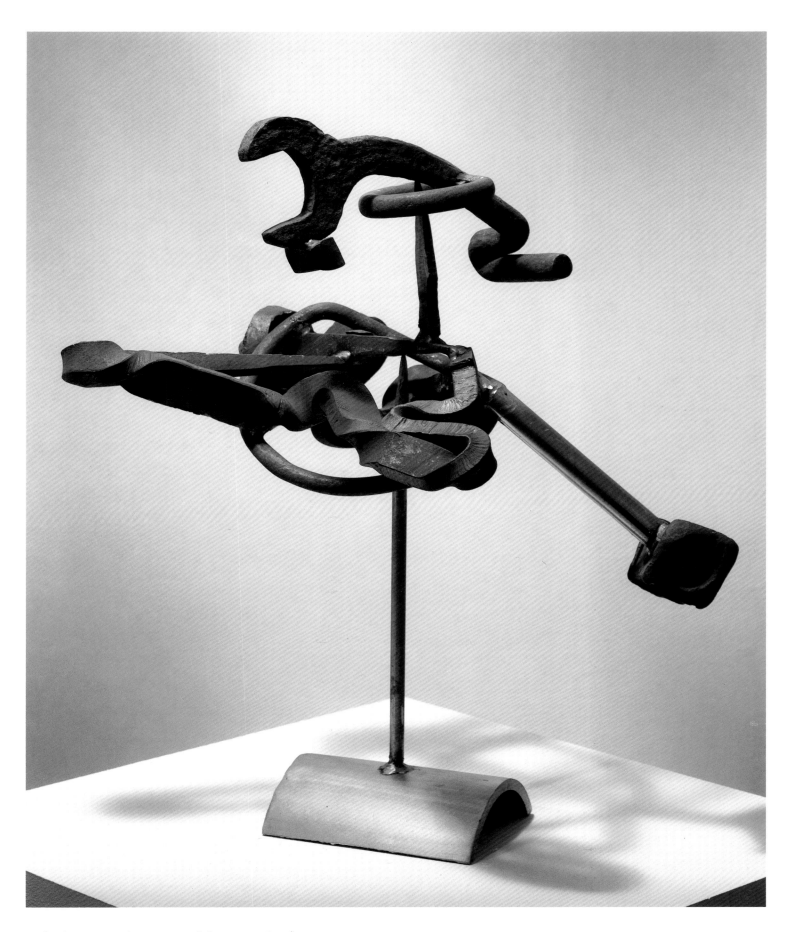

Toolpath, 1990. Steel. 25 x 22 x 15" (64 x 56 x 38 cm)

THE HAND THAT SIGNED THE PAPER
FELLED A CITY

The hand that signed the paper felled a city;
Five sovereign fingers taxed the breath,
Doubled the globe of dead and halved a country;
These five kings did a king to death.

The mighty hand leads to a sloping shoulder,
The finger joints are cramped with chalk;
A goose's quill has put an end to murder
That put an end to talk.

The hand that signed the treaty bred a fever,
And famine grew, and locusts came;
Great is the hand that holds dominion over
Man by a scribbled name.

The five kings count the dead but do not soften
The crusted wound nor stroke the brow;
A hand rules pity as a hand rules heaven;
Hands have no tears to flow.

DYLAN THOMAS

Octo, 1990. Steel. 29 x 14 x 18 ³/₄" (74 x 36 x 48 cm)

LE CANCRE

Il dit non avec la tête

mais il dit oui avec le coeur

il dit oui à ce qu'il aime

il dit non au professeur

il est debout

on le questionne

et tous les problèmes sont posés

soudain le fou rire le prend

et il efface tout

les chiffres et les mots

les dates et les noms

les phrases et les pièges

et malgré les menaces du maître

sous les huées des enfants prodiges

avec des craies de toutes les couleurs

sur le tableau noir du malheur

il dessine le visage du bonheur.

THE DUNCE

He says no with his head

but he says yes with his heart

he says yes to what he loves

he says no to the teacher

he stands

he is questioned

and all the problems are posed

sudden laughter seizes him

and he erases all

the words and figures

names and dates

sentences and snares

and despite the teacher's threats

to the jeers of infant prodigies

with chalk of every color

on the blackboard of misfortune

he draws the face of happiness.

JACQUES PRÉVERT

Homage to Tailors, 1990. Steel. 24 x 14¹⁄₂ x 35" (61 x 37 x 89 cm)

THE TORRENT LEAVES

Rise up nimbly and go on your strange journey

to the ocean of meanings where you became one of those.

From one terrace to another through clay banks,

washing your wings with watery silt,

follow your friends. The pitcher breaks.

You're in the moving river. Living Water,

how long will you make clay pitchers

that have to be broken to enter you?

The torrent knows it can't stay on this mountain.

Leave and don't look away from the Sun as you go.

Through him you are sometimes crescent, sometimes full.

RUMI

Towanda, 1991. Steel & stainless steel. 41 ¹/₄ x 50 ¹/₄ x 36 ³/₄" (105 x 128 x 93 cm)

A POISON TREE

I was angry with my friend;
I told my wrath, my wrath did end.
I was angry with my foe:
I told it not, my wrath did grow.

And I waterd it in fears,
Night & morning with my tears:
And I sunned it with smiles,
And with soft deceitful wiles.

And it grew both day and night.
Till it bore an apple bright.
And my foe beheld it shine,
And he knew that it was mine.

And into my garden stole,
When the night had veild the pole;
In the morning glad I see;
My foe outstretched beneath the tree.

WILLIAM BLAKE

from ARIETTES OUBLIÉES

III

     "Il pleut doucement sur la ville."
               Arthur Rimbaud

Il pleure dans mon coeur
Comme il pleut sur la ville,
Quelle est cette langueur
Qui pénètre mon coeur?

O bruit doux de la pluie
Par terre et sur les toits!
Pour un coeur qui s'ennuie,
O le chant de la pluie!

Il pleure sans raison
Dans ce coeur qui s'écoeure.
Quoi! nulle trahison?
Ce deuil est sans raison.

C'est bien la pire peine
De ne savoir pourquoi,
Sans amour et sans haine,
Mon coeur a tant de peine!

from SONGS FORGOTTEN

III

     "It rains gently on the town."
               Arthur Rimbaud

It weeps in my heart
as it rains on the town.
What languorous hurt
thus pierces my heart?

Oh, sweet sound of rain
on the earth and the roofs!
For a heart dulled with pain,
oh, the song of the rain!

It weeps without reason
in my disheartened heart.
What! there's no treason?
This grief's without reason.

It's far the worst pain
not to know why,
without love or disdain,
my heart has such pain.

PAUL VERLAINE

Preceding pages and above: *Les Masques du Livre (Masks of the Book)*, 1990. Steel. 58 x 67 x 37 ³/₄" (147 x 170 x 96 cm)

ALEZ VOUS ANT, ALLEZ, ALÉS

Alez vous ant, allez, alés,
Soussy, Soing et Merencolie,
Me cuidez vous, toute ma vie,
Gouverner, comme fait avés?

Je vous prometz que non ferés,
Raison aura sur vous maistrie.
Alez [vous ant, allez, alés,
Soussy, Soing et Merencolie!]

Se jamais plus vous retournés
Avecques vostre compaignie,
Je pri a Dieu qu'il vous maudie,
Et ce par qui vous revendrés:
Alez [vous ant, allez, alés,
Soussy, Soing et Merencolie!]

O GO AWAY, AWAY, AWAY

O go away, away, away!
Melancholy, Grief, and Strife.
Think that you'll rule me all my life
The way you've done in other days?

I promise you: this will not be.
Reason will gain the mastery.
Away, away! O go away,
Melancholy, Grief, and Strife!

And if you ever do come back,
I pray that God may send a pox
On all your wretched, cursed pack,
And stifle all that gives you life.
O go away, away, away!
Melancholy, Grief, and Strife!

CHARLES D'ORLÉANS

Le Noeud de la Fortune (The Knot of Fortune), 1990. Steel & stainless steel plate. $36\,^{1}/_{4}$ x 41 x $30\,^{1}/_{2}$" (93 x 104 x 78 cm)

HOMENAJE A CLAUDIO PTOLOMEO
(Antología Palatina 9.577)

Soy hombre: poco duro

y es enorme la noche.

Pero miro hacia arriba:

las estrellas escriben.

Sin entender comprendo:

también soy escritura

y en este mismo instante

alguien me deletrea.

HOMAGE TO CLAUDIUS PTOLEMY
(Palatine Anthology 9.577)

I am a man: little do I last

and the night is enormous.

But I look up:

the stars write.

Unknowing I understand:

I too am written,

and at this very moment

someone spells me out.

OCTAVIO PAZ

Oaxaca, 1992. Steel. 14'9" x 16'5" x 6'7" (4.5 x 5 x 2 m)

from THE MAN WITH THE BLUE GUITAR

A tune beyond us as we are,
Yet nothing changed by the blue guitar;

Ourselves in the tune as if in space,
Yet nothing changed, except the place

Of things as they are and only the place
As you play them, on the blue guitar,

Placed, so, beyond the compass of change,
Perceived in a final atmosphere;

For a moment final, in the way
The thinking of art seems final when

The thinking of god is smoky dew.
The tune is space. The blue guitar

Becomes the place of things as they are,
A composing of senses of the guitar.

WALLACE STEVENS

For Chris, 1991. Steel. 11'3" x 16' x 10'3" (3.4 x 4.8 x 3.1 m)

Boxcar Hokusai, 1992. Steel. 27 ¹/₂" x 16" x 32" (69.9 x 40.6 x 81.3 cm)

D.N.A. Info, 1991. Steel. 7' x 3'7" x 5'8" (2.1 x 1.1 x 1.7 m)

WHEN YOU ARE OLD

When you are old and grey and full of sleep,
And nodding by the fire, take down this book,
And slowly read, and dream of the soft look
Your eyes had once, and of their shadows deep;

How many loved your moments of glad grace,
And loved your beauty with love false or true,
But one man loved the pilgrim soul in you,
And loved the sorrows of your changing face;

And bending down beside the glowing bars,
Murmur, a little sadly, how Love fled
And paced upon the mountains overhead
And hid his face amid a crowd of stars.

W. B. YEATS

Han, 1991. Steel. 76½ x 53 x 53" (194 x 135 x 135 cm)

Hew, 1990. Steel. 23 x 90 ¹/₂ x 35" (58 x 230 x 89 cm)

Memories, 1992. Steel & stainless steel. 15 x 16 x 16" (38 x 41 x 41 cm)

Waythrough, 1990. Steel. 21 ¹/₂ x 27 ¹/₂ x 23" (55 x 70 x 58 cm)

For Oliver, 1992. Steel. 13 ¹/₂ x 11 x 8" (34 x 28 x 20 cm)

Above: *Rigel,* 1992. Steel & stainless steel. 24 x 26 x 19¹/₂" (61 x 66 x 49.5 cm)

Below: *Chip Off the Old Block,* 1992. Steel. 20 x 20¹/₂ x 12" (51 x 52 x 30.4 cm)

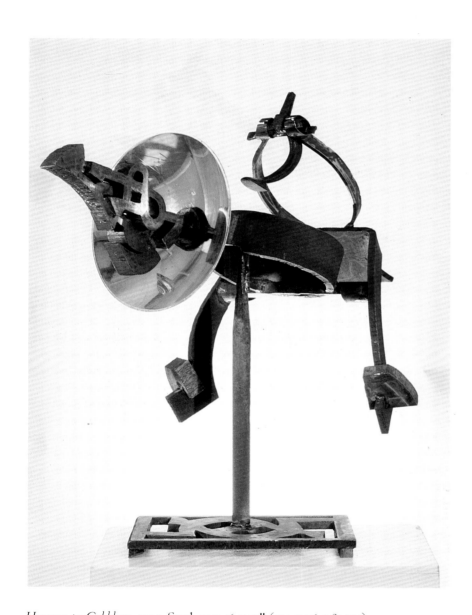

Homage to Cobblers, 1992. Steel. 51 x 46 x 32" (129 x 116 x 81 cm)

Page 2, 1992. Steel. 35 x 36 x 19" (89 x 91 x 48 cm)

Following pages: *Réves des Signes, Chalon sur Saóne*

HOW DARK AND SINGLE...

how dark and single,where he ends,the earth
(whose texture feels of pride and loneliness
alive like some dream giving more than all
life's busy little dyings may possess)

how sincere large distinct and natural
he comes to his disappearance;as a mind
full without fear might faithfully lie down
to so much sleep they only understand

enormously which fail—look:with what ease
that bright how plural tide measures her guest
(as critics will upon a poet feast)

meanwhile this ghost goes under,his drowned girth
are mountains;and beyond all hurt of praise
the unimaginable night not known

e. e. cummings

[Sculptor's dedication: For my old buddy and my teacher Roscoe]

Preceding pages: *Petaluma Studio.*
Opposite: *For Lady Day,* 1991. Lithography, Trial Proof.
Printed and published by Franck Bordas. 47 x 32" (119.4 x 81.3 cm)

Cindy Day

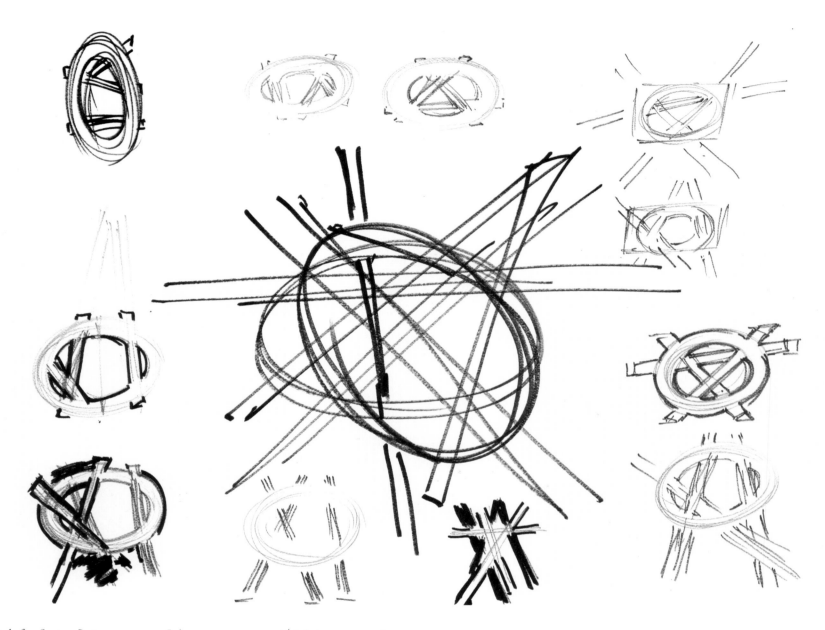

Sketch for *Spring Rain.* 1990-1992. Ink on paper. 30 x 22 ¹/₂" (76.2 x 57.2 cm)

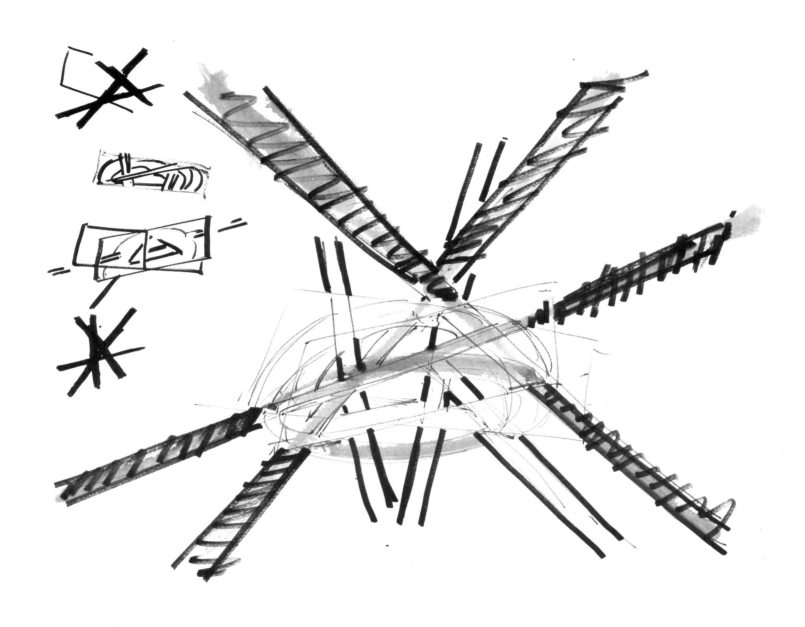

Sketch for *Spring Rain.* 1990-1992. Ink on paper. 30 x 22" (76.2 x 55.9 cm)

Following pages: *For Marianne Moore,* 1991. Lithography, Trial Proof. Printed and published by Franck Bordas. 47 x 32" (119.4 x 81.3 cm)

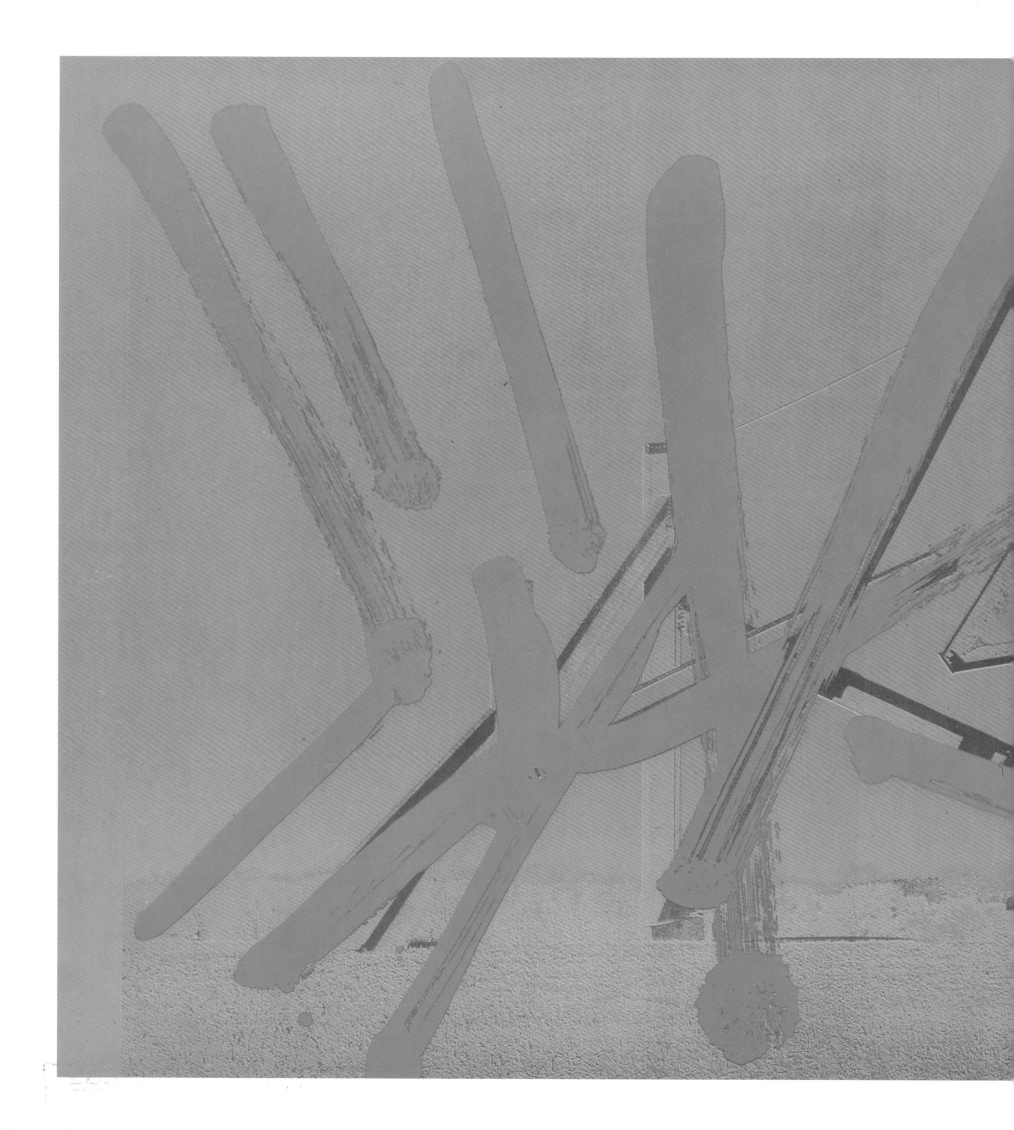

WHAT ARE YEARS?

What is our innocence,
what is our guilt? All are
    naked, none is safe. And whence
is courage, the unanswered question,
the resolute doubt,-
dumbly calling, deafly listening - that
in misfortune, even death,
    encourages others
    and in its defeat, stirs

    the soul to be strong? He
sees deep and is glad, who
    accedes to mortality
and in his imprisonment rises
upon himself as
the sea in a chasm, struggling to be
free and unable to be,
    in its surrendering
    finds its continuing.

    So he who strongly feels,
behaves. The very bird,
    grown taller as he sings, steels
his form straight up. Though he is captive,
his mighty singing
says, satisfaction is a lowly
thing, how pure a thing is joy.
    This is mortality,
    this is eternity.

MARIANNE MOORE

Untitled. 1990-1992. Ink on paper. 30 x 22" (76.2 x 55.9 cm)

Untitled. 1990–1992. Ink on paper. 30 x 22" (76.2 x 55.9 cm)

Untitled. 1990-1992. Ink on computer paper. 20 x 26" (50.8 x 66 cm)

Sketch for *Johnny Appleseed*. 1990-1992. Ink on paper. 11 x 13³/₄" (27.9 x 34.9 cm)

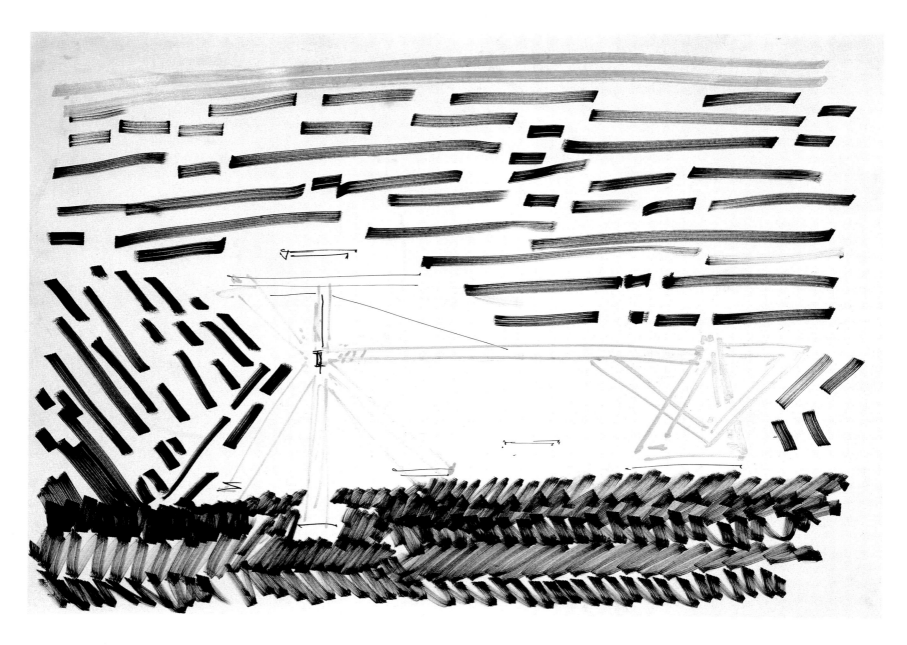

Untitled. 1990-1992. Ink on paper. 40 x 29" (101.6 x 73.7 cm)

Untitled. 1990-1992. Ink on paper. 40 x 29" (101.6 x 73.7 cm)

Hopesoup. 1990. Steel & stainless steel. 11' x 14'8" x 7'6" (3.4 x 4.5 x 2.3 m)

Dream Come True. 1990. Steel & stainless steel. 51 x 48 x 48" (1.3 x 1.2 x 1.2 m)   *Kelpswim.* 1988-1990. Stainless steel. 29 x 18 x 17" (74 x 46 x 43 cm)

Untitled. 1990. Steel & stainless steel. 19 ³/₄ x 26 x 10 ¹/₂" (50 x 66 x 27 cm)

Plorg. 1990. Steel & stainless steel. 19 ⅝ x 34 x 22 ½" (49 x 86 x 57 cm)

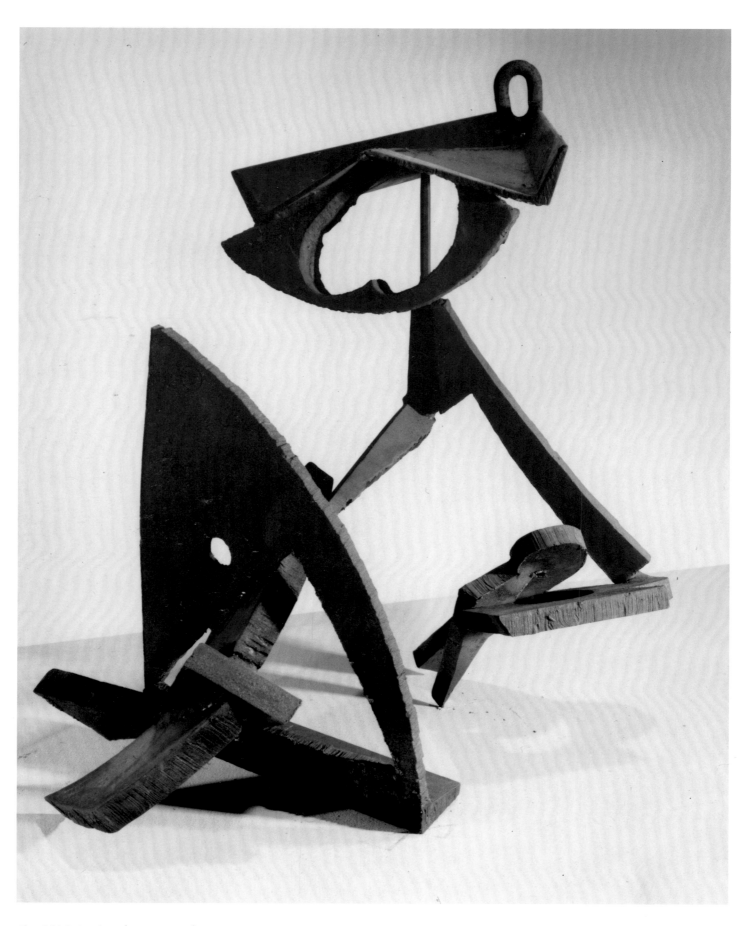

Ibu. 1991. Steel. 31 ¹/₂ x 32 x 24¹/₂" (80 x 81 x 62 cm)

For Dylan Thomas. 1991. Steel. 40 ¹/₂ x 21 x 21" (103 x 53 x 53 cm)

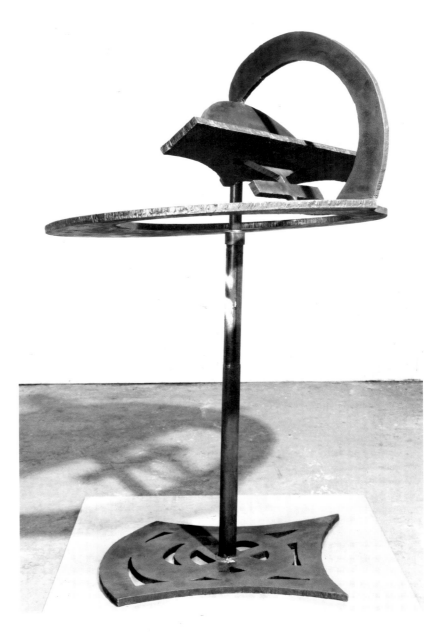

Han, 1991. Steel. 76 ½ x 53 x 53" (194 x 135 x 135 cm)

Ithaca. 1991. Steel & stainless steel. 30 $^1/_4$ x 56 $^3/_4$ x 24 $^3/_4$" (77 x 144 x 63 cm)

Thule. 1991. Welded stainless steel. 34 x 27 x 18 ¹/₄" (86 x 69 x 46 cm)

Model for Beethoven. 1991. Steel. 18 x 18 x 14 ¹/₂" (45.7 x 45.7 x 36.8 cm)

La Clef qui Tourne. 1992. Steel & stainless steel. 28 x 18 x 22" (71 x 46 x 56 cm)

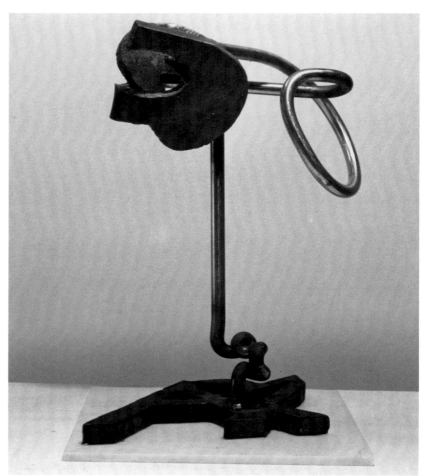

Untitled. 1992. Steel & stainless steel. 33 ¹/₂ x 35 x 28" (85 x 89 x 71 cm)

Untitled. 1992. Steel & stainless steel. 18 x 16 x 9" (46 x 41 x 23 cm)

Dodeine. 1992. Steel. 32 ¹/₄ x 27 ¹/₂ x 23 ⁵/₈" (82 x 70 x 60 cm)

Allumette. 1992. Steel. 30 x 46 x 45" (76 x 113 x 119 cm)

Leopardi. 1992. Stainless steel. 44" high (122 cm), base: 31 x 46⁷/₈" (79 x 119 cm)

Untitled. 1990. Steel. 24 x 28 x 15 ¹/₄" (61 x 71 x 39 cm)

Rescue Ring. 1980–1990. Steel. 15 x 24 x 10" (38.1 x 61 x 34.5 cm)

Following pages: *Untitled.* 1990-1992. Ink on computer paper. 33 x 18¹/₄" (83.8 x 46.4 cm)

ARCHAÏSCHER TORSO APOLLOS

Wir kannten nicht sein unerhörtes Haupt,
darin die Augenäpfel reiften. Aber
sein Torso glüht noch wie ein Kandelaber,
in dem sein Schauen, nur zurückgeschraubt,

sich hält und glänzt. Sonst könnte nicht der Bug
der Brust dich blenden, und im leisen Drehen
der Lenden könnte nicht ein Lächeln gehen
zu jener Mitte, die die Zeugung trug.

Sonst stünde dieser Stein entstellt und kurz
unter der Schultern durchsichtigem Sturz
und flimmerte nicht so wie Raubtierfelle;

und bräche nicht aus allen seinen Rändern
aus wie ein Stern: denn da ist keine Stelle,
die dich nicht sieht. Du mußt dein Leben ändern.

TORSO OF AN ARCHAIC APOLLO

Never will we know his fabulous head
where the eyes' apples slowly ripened. Yet
his torso glows: a candelabrum set
before his gaze which is pushed back and hid,

restrained and shining. Else the curving breast
could not thus blind you, nor through the soft turn
of the loins could this smile easily have passed
into the bright groins where the genitals burned,

Else stood this stone a fragment and defaced,
with lucent body from the shoulders falling,
too short, not gleaming like a lion's fell;

nor would this star have shaken the shackles off,
bursting with light, until there is no place
that does not see you. You must change your life.

RAINER MARIA RILKE

INDEX

First published in the United States of America in 1993
by Rizzoli International Publications, Inc.,
300 Park Avenue South, New York, NY 10010
© 1993 by Rizzoli International Publications, Inc.
All rights reserved. No part of this publication may be reproduced in any manner
whatsoever without written permission from Rizzoli International Publications, Inc.
Images © 1993 by Mark di Suvero. All rights reserved.

Published on the occasion of *Mark di Suvero: Sculpture*, April 24 - June 12, 1993 at
Gagosian Gallery, 136 Wooster Street, New York, NY 10012

Cataloging-in-Publication Data for this book is available from the Library of Congress
ISBN: 0-8478-1771-7

This volume is the ninth in a series of Gagosian Gallery/Rizzoli publications
Series editor: Raymond Foye
Editorial consultant: Monroe Denton
Gagosian Gallery Coordinator: Robert Pincus-Witten
Oil & Steel Gallery Project Coordinators: Denise Corley, Jeannie Blake
Mark di Suvero Crew: Kate Levin, Lowell McKegney, Matteo Martignoni, Ivana Mestrovic
Space/Time Coordinator: Enrico Martignoni
Special thanks to Richard Bellamy

Photography credits (by page number)
Muriel Anssens: 29
John Back: 61
George Bellamy: 7, 11, 13, 14, 17, 18, 20, 23, 27, 28, 30, 35, 36, 39, 40, 41, 48, 50, 57, 63, 71, 72,
77, 90 (both), 94, 108, 111, 113 (left), 114, 116, 118 (both), 122
Peter Bellamy: Frontis, 24, 25, 47, 67, 81, 85, 110, 112, 113 (right)
D. James Dee: 96, 100, 104, 106, 107, 124
Domonique Evraid: 92
Lee Fatheree: 52, 53, 55, 56, 82
Barbara Flynn: 9
Brian Forest: 89
Lowell McKegney: 117
William Nettles: 83, 87
Pierre Plattier: 75, 79, 91 (both), 119, 120, 121
Stephen Sloman: 33, 43, 44, 45
Tom Vinetz: 59, 65, 69, 86, 88

Designed by Tony Morgan/Step Graphics Inc. New York
Production: Lisa Yee
Typeset in Monotype Centaur by Step Graphics
Printed by Virginia Lithograph

Acknowledgments
Every effort has been made to trace copyright holders of material in this book. Grateful
acknowledgment is made to the following publishers, translators, and poets:

Farrar Straus Giroux for "La Aurora" by Federico García Lorca, translation © 1988 by the
Lorca Estate and Greg Simon and Steven F. White; Harper Collins Publishers for a selec-
tion from *The Way of Life* by Lao Tzu, translation © 1944, 1972 by Witter Bynner;
Threshold Books for "Unmarked Boxes" and "The Torrent Leaves" by Rumi, translation
© 1984 by John Moyne and Coleman Barks; Harvard University Press for "Sonnet 165" by
Sor Juana Inés de la Cruz, translated by Margaret Sayers Peden; Laura S. King for her
translation of "Truth: Balade De Bon Conseyl" by Geoffrey Chaucer, © 1993; Miles
Bellamy for his translations of "Drinking Alone Under the Moon" by Li Po © 1991, and an
excerpt from "Canto I" by Dante, © 1993; University of California Press for translations of
"Abend" and "Archaïscher Torso Apollos" by Rainer Maria Rilke, translated by C.F.
MacIntyre, © 1940 by C.F. MacIntyre, and, "It pleut doucement sur la ville" by Paul
Verlaine, translated by C.F. MacIntyre, © 1948 by University of California Press; New
Directions Publishing Corporation for "The Force that Through the Green Fuse Drives
the Flower" and "The Hand That Signed the Paper Felled a City" by Dylan Thomas, ©
1952, 1953 by Dylan Thomas, and, "La Calle" and "Homenaje a Claudio Ptolomeo" by
Octavio Paz, translated by Muriel Rukeyser and Eliot Weinberger, respectively, © 1963,
1973 Octavio Paz and Muriel Rukeyser, © 1979 by Octavio Paz and Eliot Weinberger;
Macmillan Publishing Co., Inc., for "To A Friend Whose Work Has Come to Nothing"
and "When You Are Old" by William Butler Yeats, © 1931, 1934 by W.B. Yeats, ©
renewed 1956, 1957 by Bertha Georgie Yeats, published in *The Poems of W. B. Yeats: A New
Edition*, edited by Richard J. Finneran, and, "What Are Years?" by Marianne Moore, published in *Collected Poems*, © 1941, 1969; City Lights Books for "Le Cancre" by Jacques Prévert,
translation © 1958 by Lawrence Ferlinghetti; James J. Wilhelm for his translation of "Alez
vous ant, allez, alés" by Charles d'Orléans, © 1990; Vintage Books for a selection from
"The Man With the Blue Guitar" by Wallace Stevens, © 1954, 1982 by Wallace Stevens
and Holly Stevens, published in *Collected Poems*; Little, Brown Publishers for "Of all the
Sounds despatched abroad" by Emily Dickinson, published in *Collected Poems*; Harcourt
Brace Jovanovich for "how dark and single" by e.e. cummings, © 1954, 1988 by e.e. cummings, published in *Collected Poems*.